PEEKABOO!
I LOVE YOU!

by Bil Keane

FAWCETT GOLD MEDAL • NEW YORK

A Fawcett Gold Medal Book

Published by Ballantine Books

ISBN 0-449-12824-5

This edition published by arrangement with The Register & Tribune Syndicate, Inc.

Printed in Canada

First Canadian Printing: May 1984

First Fawcett Gold Medal Edition: May 1971
First Ballantine Books Edition: April 1983
Second Printing: August 1984

"It's a sweater. You have to wear it when Mommy starts getting chilly."

"I wish we'd get our old carpet back so we could eat in the livin' room again."

"You're lucky, Mommy. You get to do REAL cleaning and ironing and cooking and..."

"How many more days 'til it snows?"

"Anyhow, we had ice cream from the--stop that
smilin', Dolly--from the ice cream man and you
guys didn't!"

"Daddy, 28 plus (36 plus 49) equals (28 plus 36)
plus what—using the associative principle?"

"It's the sitter who lets us stay up to watch
Johnny Carson!"

"No, no, Daddy! They're for Billy's school party."

"Barfy! Dinner!"

"In school today we learned how to loot the flag
and take the pledge."

"Anyhow, Grandma, he's SMILING at you!"

"I was elected president of the second grade!
My job is to see that the floor is kept clean."

"You've heard Billy speak of old Mrs. Gallagher?
THAT'S old Mrs. Gallagher."

"Do I have to get washed? Tomorrow isn't a school day."

"Are you going to cry if I win?"

"Will you tell Daddy not to talk too long? Debbie
said she might call me up today."

"Don't turn the page, Mommy, we're not finished readin' this one yet."

"Watch out, everybody! You'll get hair-sprayed!"

"Now that the house is cleaned and straightened
for the baby sitter, it'd be kind of nice
to stay home."

"Rich man, poor man, beggar man, THIEF!"

"Nobody's allowed in the house 'til Mommy finds
the diamond that fell out of her ring!"

"Grandma says not to worry about finding the diamond you lost 'cause she'll say a prayer to St. Anthony."

"I'll take care of looking all around here in front
of the TV set."

"Does losin' the diamond out of your ring mean
you're not engaged to Daddy any more!"

"Don't worry, Mommy, if you don't find the diamond by Christmas, Santa will bring you another one."

"Mommy! I just took something shiny out of PJ's mouth and it's your diamond!"

"I'll race you!"

"Children! For heaven's sake! We'll only be
five minutes!"

"Maybe it'll stop this time, this time, this time..."

"We put a chair there so Daddy won't roll off."

"Does this say 'Dear Grandma, how are you'?"

"What's his name?"

"How many more days 'til Santa does his thing?"

"...And a cartridge in a bare tree."

"Miss Helen, how do I spell my last name?"

"On, Comet! On, Cupid! On, Donder
and Nixon!"

"Mommy, are ALL these people going to see
Santa Claus?"

" "Member when Mommy phoned you 'cause
I scribbled on the wall? Well, that
was a mistake--Jeffy did it."

"We've run out of hiding places at home."

"Can I bake a birthday cake for Jesus now?"

"I ate so much Daddy can't even lift me!"

"They want to talk to my FATHER."

"Grandma's on the phone, Daddy. She wants to wish you a happy New Year."

"But I KNOW I hurt it someplace right around that knee."

"I told Miss Helen I'd stay and help her, but she doesn't need any help."

"Daddy says it's very good and he's holding it
upside-down!"

"I KNEW this was our morning for the car pool
when I saw it snowing!"

"But, it smells just like summer when we're
on vacation!"

"Anyhow, I kept MYSELF clean, Mommy."

"I know who he is! That's the man who makes
all the pennies!"

"Don't look, Mommy, don't look!"

"Sing some more, Daddy! Mommy's ladies are
in the living room and they're all clapping!"

"Will sucking on that piece of glass help make Billy better?"

"Hi, Daddy! Did you bring home something else
for Billy to play with?"

"Your tray! Here comes your tray! Guess what
it is--it's soup again!"

"No fair! Last time I was sick I had to stay in my bedroom!"

"Maybe if you call Grandma and tell her about my sore finger she'd send ME a get well card, too."

"Mommy! Billy's feeling his old self again! He's
fightin' with everybody!"

"Hi, Mommy! I 'vited Debbie's mother in for a
cup of tea. She wants to meet you."

"Why do you always taste the thread first?"

"Daddy, come over to the mirror so you can see
my dirty face."

"PJ sneezed and made a splash on me!"

"Mommy's dressing her ears, too. That means we're not going."

"Don't be a dummy, Jeffy! The Easter Bunny doesn't come down the chimney--he comes in the front door."

"The clothes are dry, Mommy. I felt them all."

"I can get my own drink!"

"We beat you, Mommy! We beat!"

"All right, you have two pieces of candy. Now, if I give you four more how many will you have?"

"Mommy, Joan of Arc was Noah's wife,
wasn't she?"

"Wait a minute, Daddy, Red Riding Hood didn't go to the Three Bears' house—that was Goldilocks!"

"Mommy! Guess whose happy birthday it is!
Did I get any bigger?"

"Oh, those are only LITTLE presents. I'll open them last."

"I HAD to lick it first. It was dusty."

"Your lunch, Daddy! You forgot your lunch!"

"Mommy! The washer is going like this: hop, hop, hop..."

"The Romper Room lady says she sees me an' I'm
still in my 'jammies!"

"Hi, dear. The children all left today on a rocket trip to the moon."   "APRIL FOOL!"

"Hi, Grandma! This is me! . . . No . . . It's ME!"

"Didn't get you out of bed, did I?"

"Tan't see me!"

"If you come and pick me up right away, Mommy,
I'll get the prize for bein' the first to go home."

"The kind of people I like best are the ones that don't kiss you too much."

"I'll say 'please'!"

"You can't hang your coat up in the closet. Mommy
threw all the toys in there when your car drove up."

"I'll do my own, Dolly—I don't like your cooking."

"Well, see, he hurt himself and his mommy is kissing it better."

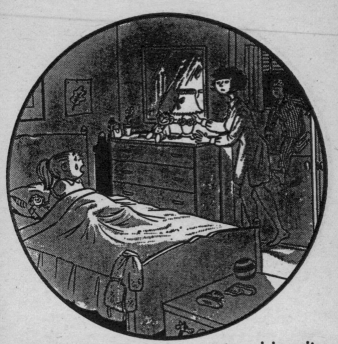

"Miss Helen changed our seats and I can't
remember where I sit!"

"If one of US spilled it, Mommy wouldn't be
smiling--she'd be mad!"

"Here's your Mother's Day card, Mommy. Miss
Johnson gave me a C for it."

"I forget, Mommy. Do we do things for YOU on Mother's Day, or is that the day you do things for US?"

"Shh! Don't call them you-know-whats in front of Barfy."

"Why do we look down to pray when God's up
THAT way?"

"Today was a real FUN day! The bus broke down
and the police had to come and help us WALK
to school!"

"I tied my right shoe, Mommy. Can you tie my
WRONG one?"

"On your mark. . . get set. . . GO!"

"Why are you painting the corn yellow?"

"Today Jeffy washed and I dried."

"We found the kitchen and bedroom, but where's
the livin' room and the bathroom?"

"PLEASE? Can't we practice sleeping in the camper tonight?"

"Ninety cents, please. The lady at your back door just bought six."

"This is a GOOD camping spot! Can we just stay here?"

"Which way to Smokey the Bear?"

"THERE it is! I see it! I see the lake!"

"Where can I ride my skateboard?"

"Those guys are lucky! They get to sleep in a TENT!"

"Why does Daddy just like to sit and LOOK at the water all day?"

"Mommy! Daddy! Will you keep talking so we
can tell you're still out there?"

"This is a NEAT house, Mommy! I wish we could live here ALL the time!"

"Boy! Are we lucky it rained! This is the best
part of the whole camping trip!"

"Our mommy's sick and tired of tryin' to cook
meals in that camper!"

"...then we ran out of gas twice, and PJ got stung by a bee, and I got ivy poison and Jeffy's sunburn blistered, and Dolly got carsick...it was a NEAT vacation!"

"Say when."   "When."

"Mommy, why do you always wave your arms and say 'abracadabra' before you start to iron?"

"Can you turn your fire around, Daddy, so the
smoke won't get in my eyes?"

"I AM real thirsty, but not for WATER!"

"That's not the way, Mommy. You have to
CRAWL to push it!"

"Did Daddy get all the parts back in the right place?"

"I don't see any big ears, do you?"

"I can't hear you, Grandma! Can you turn up the volume?"

"Is it okay if I get out of the tub now?"

"No, Cathy, my mommy says I don't want to
come over right now."

"One... two... three... fourteen... sixty...
thirty... hundred! Here I come, ready or not!"

"Our Daddy said you have a phobia. Can we see it?"

"Did you call me, Mommy?"